? Essential Question
What do good problem solvers do?

THE Bill OF Rights

BY JANE KELLEY

Introduction

Imagine that you lived during colonial times. You had to follow English laws and obey the English king. You thought many of the laws were unfair and the taxes you had to pay were too high. If you protested or refused to pay taxes, you could be put in jail!

The colonists were happy to be free after they won the American Revolution. However, they had a lot of decisions to make. Who would lead the country and make the laws?

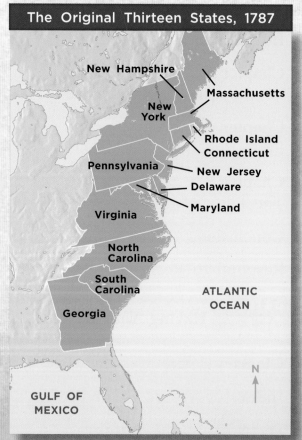

The Original Thirteen States, 1787

New Hampshire

Massachusetts

New York

Rhode Island
Connecticut

Pennsylvania

New Jersey

Delaware

Maryland

Virginia

North Carolina

South Carolina

Georgia

ATLANTIC OCEAN

N

GULF OF MEXICO

CHAPTER 1
Who Speaks for the People?

In the summer of 1787, a big meeting, called a convention, was held in Philadelphia. Twelve of the 13 states sent **delegates**, people they chose to represent them. The delegates had to agree on how to form a new government. The situation was challenging. The country was still recovering from the war. They didn't want a new government to take away any of their hard-won freedom.

There were many speeches at the convention. The delegates didn't always agree, and sometimes they were forced to find a way to work through their differences and **compromise**. This took all summer.

On September 17, 1787, the delegates voted on a new plan for the government, called the Constitution. They needed the states to approve the proposal. If 9 of the 13 states (or two-thirds) approved the Constitution, the new government could begin. If they didn't approve it, the new union could fall apart.

The states were all different. Some states wanted a strong government to lead the country. Other states wanted greater freedom to make their own decisions.

People who wanted a strong central government were called **Federalists**. The word *federal* describes a central government where states still have control of some laws. Many Federalists were business owners who thought that having a strong central government would help the economy grow.

Alexander Hamilton was a founder of the Federalist Party.

(bkgd) Photodisc/Getty Images; (b) Library of Congress Prints and Photographs Division [LC-DIG-pomsca-17523]

Another group was the **Anti-Federalists**. Many Anti-Federalists were wealthy landowners or farmers who valued their states' **independence**. They thought the Constitution gave too much power to the federal government. They wanted the states to have more power over their own laws.

"I know of no way of judging...the future but by the past," said Patrick Henry, an Anti-Federalist, in 1775.

The states debated the Constitution. Delaware was the first state to **ratify**, or approve, the Constitution. New Jersey and Georgia soon followed. These states had small populations. The Constitution gave each state an equal vote in the **Senate**, no matter how many people lived in the state.

The Federalists and Anti-Federalists in Virginia and New York could not agree.

Patrick Henry, a leading Anti-Federalist in Virginia, insisted that the Constitution needed a bill of rights.

James Madison, a Federalist, came to the rescue. He suggested a compromise. He promised that if Virginia ratified the Constitution, and elected him to Congress, he would work on adding a bill of rights to the Constitution. Madison's promise convinced Virginia to ratify the Constitution.

James Madison is called the Father of the Constitution. His willingness to compromise made forming the new government possible.

Other states had not voted on the Constitution yet. In New York, the Federalists and Anti-Federalists used newspapers to spread their message. Alexander Hamilton, and other Federalists, argued that a national bill of rights was unnecessary. They thought that a strong government would do what was best for everyone. Then New York ratified the Constitution. With more than two-thirds of the states' votes, the Constitution became law.

STOP AND CHECK

Why did some states need to be convinced to vote for the Constitution?

THE

FEDERALIST:

ADDRESSED TO THE

PEOPLE OF THE STATE OF NEW-YORK.

NUMBER I.

Introduction.

AFTER an unequivocal experience of the inefficacy of the subsisting federal government, you are called upon to deliberate on a new constitution for the United States of America. The subject speaks its own importance; comprehending in its consequences, nothing less than the existence of the UNION, the safety and welfare of the parts of which it is composed, the fate of an empire, in many respects, the most interesting in the world. It has been frequently remarked, that it seems to have been reserved to the people of this country, by their conduct and example, to decide the important question, whether societies of men are really capable or not, of establishing good government from reflection and choice, or whether they are forever destined to depend, for their political constitutions, on accident and force. If there be any truth in the remark, the crisis, at which we are arrived, may with propriety be regarded as the æra in which

A   that

The *Federalist Papers* helped persuade people to support the Constitution.

CHAPTER 2
Protecting Individual Rights

The new Congress met for the first time in April 1789. The members of the **House of Representatives** formed committees to work on different issues. James Madison kept his promise to Virginians and started working on a bill of rights. Not everyone believed the bill was needed, and it took three months to get a group of representatives to meet and talk about his plan.

Amending the Constitution

The delegates who wrote the Constitution included a way to make amendments, or changes, in the future. To amend the Constitution, two-thirds of the members of Congress and three-quarters of the states must vote for the change.

Members of the committee took ideas from the Bill of Rights in the Virginia Constitution. It was hard to decide which rights to include. Finally, 12 **amendments** were approved. Now, it was the states' turn to vote.

Two years later, 10 of the 12 amendments were approved by 11 states. These amendments, known as the Bill of Rights, protect people from being treated unfairly by the government.

Not a Separate Document

The Bill of Rights does not have a title calling it *The Bill of Rights*. When people talk about the Bill of Rights, what they mean are the first ten amendments to the Constitution.

Timeline for the Bill of Rights

April 1789: James Madison introduces the Bill of Rights to the House of Representatives.

September 25, 1789: Congress sends the Bill of Rights to the states to be voted on.

November 1789: New Jersey is the first state to ratify the Bill of Rights.

December 1789: Maryland and North Carolina ratify.

January 1790: South Carolina, New Hampshire, and Delaware ratify.

February 1790: New York ratifies.

March 1790: Pennsylvania ratifies.

June 1790: Rhode Island ratifies.

November 1791: Vermont ratifies.

December 1791: Virginia ratifies.

The amendments are now part of the Constitution.

(bkgd) Photodisc/Getty Images, (c) Craig Brewer/Punchstock

STOP AND CHECK

What important role did James Madison play in the development of the Bill of Rights?

CHAPTER 3
The Bill of Rights

Members of Congress remembered fighting for their freedom from the English king when they wrote the Bill of Rights. As you read about the amendments in this chapter, can you tell which amendments were written because of the way the king treated the colonists?

Protecting Your Rights

The Declaration of Independence says that people have a right to "life, liberty, and the pursuit of happiness." What does that mean? The Bill of Rights is a list of rights that people have.

In CONGRESS. JULY 4, 1776.

The unanimous Declaration of the thirteen united States of America.

Congress shall make no law respecting an establishment of religion, or prohibiting the free exercise thereof; or abridging the freedom of speech, or of the press; or the right of the people peaceably to assemble, and to petition the Government for a redress of grievances.

This is the original text for the First Amendment. The amendments were all written in legal language, which can make them difficult to understand.

THE FIRST AMENDMENT

The First Amendment is about freedom of religion. Many colonists came to America to have religious freedom. This amendment says people can practice any religion.

The amendment also gives people the freedom to talk or write about whatever they want. People have the right to ask the government to change, and can protest without worrying that they'll get in trouble.

You have the right to meet and protest peacefully.

THE SECOND AND THIRD AMENDMENTS

The Second Amendment gives people the right to own weapons to hunt or to defend themselves. It also lets the states have a National Guard to help the regular army and to protect and help people.

During colonial times, Americans were sometimes mistreated by the English army. The army could force people to give English soldiers food or a place to sleep. The Third Amendment says that soldiers must have your permission to stay in your house.

THE FOURTH AMENDMENT

During the Revolutionary War, English soldiers could search or arrest people for no reason. The Fourth Amendment protects you from being searched without a clear reason.

English soldiers could search the colonists' houses at any time.

THE FIFTH THROUGH THE EIGHTH AMENDMENTS

If you've broken a law, you still have rights. These four amendments make sure that people accused of crimes are treated fairly.

The Fifth Amendment says a person can't be put on trial unless a grand jury says there is enough evidence. You can't be punished unless a jury says you're guilty. Also, the government can't take things that belong to you without paying for them.

These jurors are ready to hear evidence in a trial.

The Sixth Amendment gives you the right to be told what crime you've been accused of. You have the right to a trial with a jury and the right to defend yourself.

(bkgd) Photodisc/Getty Images, (b) Comstock/PunchStock

Sometimes people argue about property or money. The Seventh Amendment says you can have a trial in front of a jury to solve the disagreement.

You still have rights, even if a jury finds you're guilty of committing a crime. The Eighth Amendment prevents the government from mistreating you if you're guilty of a crime.

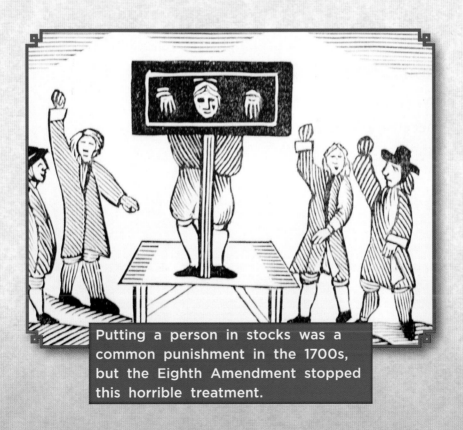

Putting a person in stocks was a common punishment in the 1700s, but the Eighth Amendment stopped this horrible treatment.

THE NINTH AND TENTH AMENDMENTS

Think of how long the Bill of Rights would be if it listed every possible right. The Ninth Amendment was a compromise that was made between the Federalists and Anti-Federalists. It solved the worry that protecting specific rights would limit how many rights people have. This amendment says that you have more rights than those in the Constitution.

The Tenth Amendment says that the states, or the people, are in charge of whatever the Constitution doesn't say Congress can do. This compromise prevents the federal government from being too powerful. Instead, the Bill of Rights limits its power.

STOP AND CHECK

What are some of the rights you have because of the Bill of Rights?

Conclusion

Over 200 years ago the Bill of Rights became part of the Constitution. The United States has changed a lot since then, and other amendments have been added to the Constitution. Do you know any of these other amendments?

The process used to develop the Bill of Rights still works. People can still discuss problems and find compromises to solve them.

The United States has the oldest written constitution that is still used. It has lasted so long because there is a way to change it. That is why our Constitution is a model for other governments. It is a constitution of the people and for the people.

These Iraqi women proudly show that they also have the right to vote.

(bkgd) Photodisc/Getty Images, (t) Photodisc/Punchstock, (b) SABAH ARAR/AFP/Getty Images

Respond to Reading

Summarize

Use important details from
The Bill of Rights to summarize
how representatives solved
problems. Your graphic
organizer may help you.

Problem	Solution

Text Evidence

1. Turn to page 10. What text feature do you see?
   What kind of text is *The Bill of Rights*? GENRE

2. How did members of the House of
   Representatives solve the problem of making
   a bill of rights? Give examples from Chapter 2.
   PROBLEM AND SOLUTION

3. What does the word *ratify* mean on page 6?
   How does the author help you figure out the
   meaning? Find another example of a definition
   or restatement in the text.
   DEFINITIONS AND RESTATEMENTS

4. Write about the problem James Madison had to
   solve in getting Virginia to ratify the Constitution.
   Explain how he solved it. WRITE ABOUT READING

Compare Texts

Read about how sharing information can help people solve problems.

Having Your Say

We can't travel back in time. However, paintings and other images can help us picture what life was like long ago. The painting below shows people reading the news of the day. Federalists and Anti-Federalists both wrote things that were published in newspapers. This was one way they shared their ideas.

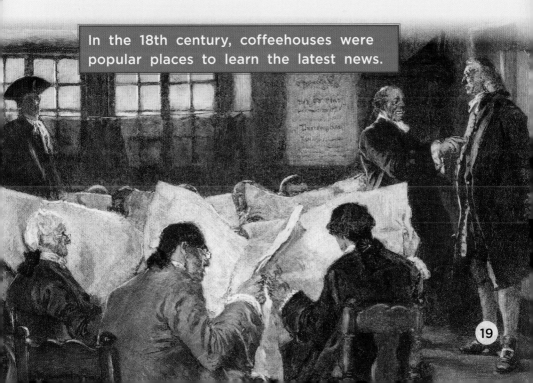

In the 18th century, coffeehouses were popular places to learn the latest news.

Compare the painting to the photo below. The people in the photo could be reading things from anywhere in the United States or even from other parts of the world.

The people could be discussing the Fourteenth Amendment. This amendment was passed after the Civil War. It said that all people who were born in the United States, including African Americans who had been enslaved, are U.S. citizens.

Maybe they are reading that women finally got the right to vote in 1920, when the Nineteenth Amendment was passed.

Some of the people here could be writing their own essays and publishing them on the Internet.

People still work to amend the Constitution. How does technology make this easier today? Now we can communicate with each other instantly, and anyone can publish ideas on the Internet. Do people have the same opportunity to resolve their differences face to face?

The people who wrote the Constitution and the Bill of Rights worked together in the same room until they could agree. Is it harder to compromise when people are not in the same room?

More amendments will be proposed and debated in the future. That's why we need to know our rights. It's a good idea to learn about new laws and to ask questions.

The Constitution and the Bill of Rights were written more than 200 years ago. We still need to tell our representatives what we think. If we don't, how can they really represent us?

Make Connections

How do reading and sharing information help solve problems? ESSENTIAL QUESTION

How do *The Bill of Rights* and *Having Your Say* show how people reach a compromise when they want different things? TEXT TO TEXT

Glossary

amendments *(uh-MEND-muhnts)* changes in wording or meaning to a law *(page 9)*

Anti-Federalists *(an-tigh-FED-uhr-uh-lists)* people who believe states should govern themselves and make their own rules *(page 5)*

compromise *(KOM-pruh-mighz)* an agreement where neither group on opposing sides gets everything it wants *(page 3)*

delegates *(DEL-i-gits)* people who are chosen to represent other people at a meeting *(page 3)*

Federalists *(FED-uhr-uh-lists)* people who believe there should be a strong central government leading the states *(page 4)*

House of Representatives *(HOWS uv rep-ri-ZEN-tuh-tivz)* the house of Congress in which the number of representatives from a state is based on population *(page 8)*

independence *(in-di-PEN-duhns)* freedom from outside control *(page 5)*

ratify *(RAT-uh-figh)* to approve *(page 6)*

Senate *(SEN-it)* the house of Congress in which each state has two representatives *(page 6)*

Index

Focus on
Social Studies

Purpose To understand the different opinions held by people in a group and to find possible compromises

What to Do

Step 1 ▶ With a partner or small group, choose an issue that affects students, such as the use of cell phones at school.

Step 2 ▶ Make a Venn diagram on a sheet of paper. Label one circle "for" and the other "against." Label the area where the circles overlap "both."

Step 3 ▶ Write reasons for and against the issue you chose in the two labeled circles. If there is a reason that is in both circles, for and against, write it in the area where the circles overlap. What compromises might you make? Make a decision about your issue.

Step 4 ▶ Share your results with the class. Explain your solution and how you reached it.